PIT BOSS Gas Griddle Cookbook for Beginners 2021

365-Day New Tasty Recipes to Enjoy Flavorful, Stress-free BBQ with Your Pit Boss Griddle

Sarmi Rony

Table of Contents

Introduction

A lot of beautiful memories are created during celebrations and events that include outdoor grills and barbecues. The smell of grilled meat in the air, combined with the feeling of being surrounded by friends and loved ones, makes for a truly remarkable gathering. Thanks to the technology used by this amazing machine—Pit Boss gas griddle, you can enjoy your favorite dishes in minutes.

This cookbook contains exclusive information on the history and operation of the Pit Boss gas griddle. It also covers recipes of meals that can be prepared with it. Keep reading to discover additional info such as features of the Pit Boss gas griddle, tips for successful barbecue, and common FAQs.

Cooking has never tasted better or been more enjoyable than with the Pit Boss gas griddle that seeks to keep families together while cooking. Learn how to enhance every flavor and recipe with the potential of your Pit Boss gas griddle and change your backyard barbecues forever.

Chapter 1: Chicken Recipes

Asian Chicken Drumsticks

Prep Time: 30 minutes

Cook Time: 45 minutes

Serve: 3

Ingredients:

- 3 lb. chicken drumsticks
- 2 teaspoons sesame oil
- 2 cloves garlic, minced
- 2 teaspoons ginger, grated
- ¼ cup brown sugar
- 2 tablespoons honey

Directions:

1. Set your Pit Boss griddle to smoke mode.
2. Preheat it to 350 degrees F or to medium heat.
3. Grill the chicken drumsticks over indirect heat for 30 minutes, flipping every 5 minutes.
4. Transfer chicken to a plate.
5. Add the sesame oil to a pan over medium heat.
6. Cook the garlic and ginger for 30 seconds.
7. Stir in the sugar and honey.
8. Cook for 3 minutes, stirring.
9. Dip the chicken in the sauce and serve.

Marinated Buttermilk Chicken

Preparation Time: 10 minutes
Cooking Time: 10 minutes
Serve: 4

Ingredients:

- 1 lb chicken breasts, boneless
- 2 tbsp butter, melted
- 1 tbsp brown sugar
- 1/2 tsp chili powder
- 2 tsp Italian seasoning
- 1 tsp onion powder
- 1 tbsp garlic, minced
- 1 1/2 cups buttermilk
- Pepper
- Salt

Directions:

1. Add chicken and remaining ingredients into the zip-lock bag. Seal bag, shake well and place in the refrigerator overnight.
2. Preheat the Pit Boss griddle to high heat.
3. Spray griddle top with cooking spray.
4. Place marinated chicken on a hot griddle top and cook for 4-5 minutes on each side.
5. Serve and enjoy.

Spicy Lime Chicken Wings

Prep Time: 1 hour and 10 minutes
Cook Time: 20 minutes
Serve: 4

Ingredients:

- 1 teaspoon chili powder
- 2 lb. chicken wings
- 2 tablespoons cilantro, chopped
- 1 teaspoon cumin
- 1 lime zest
- 1 ½ tablespoons olive oil

Directions:

1. Combine all the ingredients in a bowl.
2. Cover and refrigerate for 1 hour.
3. Preheat your Pit Boss griddle to 350 degrees F or to medium heat.
4. Grill the chicken wings for 15 to 20 minutes, flipping every 5 minutes.

Moroccan Chicken

Preparation Time: 10 minutes
Cooking Time: 10 minutes
Serve: 4

Ingredients:

- 4 chicken breasts, boneless & cut into 1-inch pieces
- 1/4 tsp turmeric
- 1/2 tsp ground cinnamon
- 1 tsp paprika
- 1 tsp ground coriander
- 1 1/2 tsp ground cumin
- 1 tbsp ginger, grated
- 1 tbsp garlic, minced
- 2 tbsp lemon juice
- 1/4 cup olive oil
- Pepper
- Salt

Directions:

1. Add chicken and remaining ingredients into the zip-lock bag. Seal bag, shake well, and place in the refrigerator overnight.
2. Preheat the Pit Boss griddle to high heat.
3. Spray griddle top with cooking spray.
4. Place marinated chicken on a hot griddle top and cook for 4-5 minutes on each side.
5. Serve and enjoy.

Chicken with Veggies

Preparation Time: 10 minutes
Cooking Time: 15 minutes
Serve: 4

Ingredients:

- 1 lb chicken breasts, boneless & cut into 1-inch pieces
- 8 oz mushrooms, sliced
- 4 oz bell pepper, cut into small pieces
- 1/2 cup onion, cut into small pieces
- 1 lb zucchini, cut into 1-inch pieces
- 1 1/2 tbsp garlic, minced
- 2 tbsp olive oil
- Pepper
- Salt

Directions:

1. Add chicken, oil, garlic, pepper, and salt into the mixing bowl and toss well. Allow marinating for 15 minutes.
2. Preheat the Pit Boss griddle to high heat.
3. Spray griddle top with cooking spray.
4. Add chicken on hot griddle top and cook for 2-3 minutes on each side.
5. Once the chicken is cooked then add veggies and sear until veggies are cooked.
6. Serve and enjoy.

Chicken & Corn Fritters

Prep Time: 15 minutes
Cook Time: 45 minutes
Serve: 8

Ingredients:

- 1 ½ lb. ground chicken
- 1 cup cheddar cheese, shredded
- 2 eggs, beaten
- ¾ cup corn kernels
- 2 teaspoons baking powder
- ¾ cup flour

Directions:

1. Preheat your Pit Boss griddle to 425 degrees F or medium high heat.
2. Combine all the ingredients in a bowl.
3. Form patties from the mixture.
4. Add the patties to the griddle.
5. Cook for 20 minutes, flipping every 5 minutes.

Buffalo Chicken Wings

Prep Time: 10 minutes
Cook Time: 25 minutes
Serve: 4

Ingredients:

- 2 lb. chicken wings
- ½ cup Pit Boss sweet heat rub
- ½ cup buffalo sauce

Directions:

1. Preheat your Pit Boss griddle to 450 degrees F or to high heat.
2. Season chicken with the rub.
3. Place on the griddle.
4. Cook for 20 minutes, flipping halfway through.
5. Brush with the buffalo sauce.
6. Cook for another 7 to 10 minutes.
7. Dip in remaining buffalo sauce before serving.

Cheesy Chicken Burger Patties

Preparation Time: 10 minutes
Cooking Time: 12 minutes
Serve: 6

Ingredients:

- 1 egg
- 2 lbs ground chicken
- 1/2 cup cheddar cheese, shredded
- 1/2 cup onion, diced
- 1 tsp garlic, minced
- 1 oz ranch seasoning
- 1/2 cup breadcrumbs
- Pepper
- Salt

Directions:

1. Add all ingredients into the mixing bowl and mix until well combined.
2. Preheat the Pit Boss griddle to medium heat.
3. Spray griddle top with cooking spray.
4. Make 6 patties from the mixture and place on hot griddle top and cook for 6-8 minutes on each side.
5. Serve and enjoy.

Stuffed Chicken Breasts

Prep Time: 15 minutes
Cook Time: 35 minutes
Serve: 4

Ingredients:

- 4 chicken breast fillets
- 3 cloves garlic, minced
- 8 oz. Italian sausage, crumbled and cooked
- 8 oz. ricotta cheese
- 8 oz. mozzarella cheese, sliced
- 2 tablespoons Italian parsley, minced

Directions:

1. Set your Pit Boss griddle to smoke mode.
2. Preheat it to 400 degrees F or medium high heat for 10 minutes.
3. Flatten the chicken with a meat mallet.
4. Mix the rest of the ingredients in a bowl.
5. Top the chicken with the mixture and roll.
6. Secure with a toothpick.
7. Add the chicken to the griddle.
8. Cook for 35 minutes, flipping 4 times.

Bacon-Wrapped Chicken Breast

Prep Time: 10 minutes
Cook Time: 30 minutes
Serve: 4

Ingredients:

- 4 chicken breast fillet
- 1 tablespoon olive oil
- 2 teaspoons garlic salt
- 1 teaspoon dried rosemary
- 8 slices bacon
- 1 tablespoon butter

Directions:

1. Preheat your Pit Boss griddle to 375 degrees F or to medium heat.
2. Brush both sides of chicken with olive oil.
3. Sprinkle with the garlic salt and rosemary.
4. Wrap 2 bacon slices per chicken breast fillet.
5. Brush with butter.
6. Place on the griddle.
7. Grill for 30 minutes, turning every 5 minutes.

Quick Peri Peri Chicken

Preparation Time: 10 minutes
Cooking Time: 16 minutes
Serve: 4

Ingredients:

- 4 chicken breasts, boneless & skinless
- 2 tsp oregano
- 2 tsp smoked paprika
- 2 lime juice
- 1 tbsp garlic, grated
- 2 tsp chili flakes
- 2 tbsp olive oil
- 1/2 tsp salt

Directions:

1. Add chicken and remaining ingredients into the bowl and mix well. Allow marinating for 2 hours.
2. Preheat the Pit Boss griddle to high heat.
3. Spray griddle top with cooking spray.
4. Place chicken on a hot griddle top and cook for 6-8 minutes on each side.
5. Serve and enjoy.

Crispy Chicken

Prep Time: 10 minutes
Cook Time: 50 minutes
Serve: 6

Ingredients:

- 1 cup cornmeal
- 1 cup flour
- 2 tablespoons chicken seasoning
- 2 eggs, beaten
- 1 cup milk
- 4 lb. chicken

Directions:

1. Preheat your Pit Boss griddle to 300 degrees F for medium low heat.
2. In a bowl, mix the cornmeal, flour and chicken seasoning.
3. In another bowl, combine the eggs and milk.
4. Dip the chicken in the eggs and then dredge with flour.
5. Add to the griddle.
6. Cook for 50 minutes, flipping every 10 minutes.

Garlic & Parmesan Chicken Wings

Prep Time: 15 minutes

Cook Time: 25 minutes

Serve: 4

Ingredients:

- 4 lb. chicken wings
- Pinch chicken seasoning
- 2 tablespoons olive oil
- 4 tablespoons butter
- 4 cloves garlic, minced
- 2 tablespoons parsley, chopped
- ½ cup Parmesan cheese, shredded

Directions:

1. Season the chicken wings with chicken seasoning.
2. Preheat the Pit Boss griddle to 400 degrees F or to medium high heat.
3. Grill the chicken wings for 20 minutes, turning 3 to 5 times.
4. In a pan over medium heat, add the olive oil and butter.
5. Cook the garlic for 30 seconds.
6. Toss the chicken wings in the garlic butter sauce.
7. Sprinkle with the parsley and Parmesan cheese and serve.

Jerk Chicken

Prep Time: 2 hours and 15 minutes
Cook Time: 20 minutes
Serve: 10

Ingredients:

- 1 teaspoon ground allspice
- ½ teaspoon ground nutmeg
- ½ teaspoon ground cinnamon
- 2 teaspoons dried thyme
- 4 cloves garlic, minced
- 2 teaspoons ginger, grated
- 1 Habanero pepper, chopped
- ¼ cup Poblano pepper, minced
- ½ cup yellow onion, minced
- ½ cup olive oil
- 2 tablespoons lemon juice
- 1/3 cup lime juice
- 2 tablespoons honey
- 1 tablespoon tamari
- 3 lb. chicken wings

Directions:

1. Combine all the ingredients except chicken in a food processor.
2. Process until smooth.
3. Transfer to a bowl.
4. Stir in chicken.
5. Cover and refrigerate for 2 hours.
6. Preheat your Pit Boss griddle to 425 degrees F or medium high heat.
7. Grill chicken for 20 minutes, flipping every 5 minutes.

Peanut Butter & Jelly Chicken

Prep Time: 2 hours and 15 minutes

Cook Time: 35 minutes

Serve: 4

Ingredients:

Sauce

- ¼ cup peanut butter
- 1 tablespoon chili sauce
- 2 tablespoons honey
- ½ cup strawberry preserves
- ¼ cup Worcestershire sauce
- 2 tablespoons brown sugar
- ½ red onion, chopped
- 1 teaspoon black pepper

Chicken

- 4 lb. chicken thigh or chicken wings

Directions:

1. Combine sauce ingredients in a bowl.
2. Transfer half to another bowl.
3. Add the chicken to one of the bowls.
4. Cover and refrigerate for 2 hours.
5. Preheat your Pit Boss griddle to 400 degrees F or medium high heat.
6. Grill the chicken for 25 to 30 minutes, turning every 5 minutes.
7. Soak the chicken in the reserved sauce before serving.

Chapter 2: Fish & Seafood Recipes

Tasty Herb Fish

Preparation Time: 10 minutes
Cooking Time: 10 minutes
Serve: 2

Ingredients:

- 1/2 lb cod fillets
- 1 egg, lightly beaten
- 1/2 tsp dried basil
- 2 tbsp breadcrumbs
- 1/4 cup Bisquick mix
- 1/8 tsp salt

Directions:

1. In a shallow dish, add the egg.
2. In a separate shallow dish, mix breadcrumbs, Bisquick mix, basil, and salt.
3. Preheat the Pit Boss griddle to high heat.
4. Spray griddle top with cooking spray.
5. Dip fish fillets with egg then coat with breadcrumb mixture.
6. Place fish fillets on a hot griddle top and cook for 8-10 minutes.
7. Serve and enjoy.

Zucchini Tuna Patties

Preparation Time: 10 minutes
Cooking Time: 10 minutes
Serve: 6

Ingredients:

- 13 oz can tuna, drained & flaked
- 1/3 cup parsley, chopped
- 2 tsp lemon juice
- 2 egg whites
- 2 eggs, lightly beaten
- 2 cups shredded zucchini, squeezed
- 3/4 cup breadcrumbs
- 1 cup onion, chopped
- Pepper
- Salt

Directions:

1. Add all ingredients into the mixing bowl and mix until well combined.
2. Preheat the Pit Boss griddle to medium heat.
3. Spray griddle top with cooking spray.
4. Make patties from mixture and place on hot griddle top and cook until golden brown from both sides.
5. Serve and enjoy.

Cajun Fish

Preparation Time: 10 minutes
Cooking Time: 8 minutes
Serve: 4

Ingredients:

- 4 white fish fillets
- 1 tbsp olive oil
- 1/4 tsp onion powder
- 1/2 tsp ground cumin
- 1/2 tsp cayenne
- 1/2 tsp oregano
- 1 tsp paprika
- 1/2 tsp pepper
- 1/2 tsp salt

Directions:

1. In a small bowl, onion powder, cumin, cayenne, oregano, paprika, pepper, and salt.
2. Brush fish fillets with oil and rub with spice mixture.
3. Preheat the Pit Boss griddle to high heat.
4. Spray griddle top with cooking spray.
5. Place fish fillets on a hot griddle top and cook for 4 minutes on each side.
6. Serve and enjoy.

Blackened Salmon

Prep Time: 15 minutes
Cook Time: 10 minutes
Serve: 4

Ingredients:

- 2 lb. salmon fillets
- 2 tablespoons olive oil
- 1 tablespoon cayenne pepper
- 4 tablespoons sweet rib rub
- 2 cloves garlic, minced

Directions:

1. Preheat your Pit Boss griddle to 350 degrees F.
2. Brush both sides of the salmon with olive oil.
3. Sprinkle with cayenne pepper, sweet rib rub and minced garlic.
4. Grill the fish for 5 minutes per side.

Quick & Delicious Halibut

Preparation Time: 10 minutes
Cooking Time: 10 minutes
Serve: 2

Ingredients:

- 2 halibut fish fillets
- 2 tsp olive oil
- 1 tsp dried thyme
- 1/2 tsp onion powder
- 3/4 tsp garlic powder
- 1 tbsp paprika
- 1/4 tsp salt

Directions:

1. In a small bowl, mix paprika, garlic powder, onion powder, thyme, and salt.
2. Brush fish fillets with oil and rub with spice mixture.
3. Preheat the Pit Boss griddle to high heat.
4. Spray griddle top with cooking spray.
5. Place fish fillets on a hot griddle top and cook for 3-5 minutes on each side.
6. Serve and enjoy.

Shrimp with Mango Salsa

Prep Time: 15 minutes

Cook Time: 6 minutes

Serve: 4

Ingredients:

- 2 lb. shrimp, peeled and deveined
- 1 teaspoon olive oil
- Salt and pepper to taste

Salsa

- 2 cups mango, chopped
- ¼ cup cucumber, chopped
- ½ red onion, minced
- 1 teaspoon lemon juice
- 1 tablespoon parsley, chopped

Directions:

1. Preheat your Pit Boss griddle to 425 degrees F.
2. Thread the shrimp onto skewers.
3. Brush with oil.
4. Season with salt and pepper.
5. Grill for 3 minutes per side.
6. Mix salsa ingredients in a bowl.
7. Serve shrimp with salsa.

Garlic Haddock

Preparation Time: 10 minutes
Cooking Time: 10 minutes
Serve: 4

Ingredients:

- 4 haddock fish fillets
- 2 tbsp garlic, minced
- 2 tbsp olive oil
- Salt

Directions:

1. Brush fish fillets with oil and season with garlic and salt.
2. Preheat the Pit Boss griddle to high heat.
3. Spray griddle top with cooking spray.
4. Place fish fillets on a hot griddle top and cook for 4-5 minutes on each side.
5. Serve and enjoy.

Grilled Lobster Tails

Prep Time: 10 minutes
Cook Time: 10 minutes
Serve: 3

Ingredients:

- ¾ stick butter, softened
- 1 clove garlic, minced
- 2 tablespoons chives, chopped
- Salt and pepper to taste
- 3 lobster tails, butterflied

Directions:

1. Set your Pit Boss to smoke.
2. Preheat your grill to 350 degrees F.
3. In a bowl, mix the butter, garlic, chives, salt and pepper.
4. Brush the lobster tails with the butter mixture.
5. Grill for 5 minutes per side.

Spicy Shrimp

Prep Time: 40 minutes

Cook Time: 6 minutes

Serve: 4

Ingredients:

- 2 cloves garlic, minced
- 2 teaspoons chili paste
- ½ teaspoon cumin
- 1 tablespoon lime juice
- ¼ teaspoon paprika
- ¼ teaspoon red pepper flakes
- 1 lb. shrimp, peeled and deveined

Directions:

1. Combine all the ingredients except shrimp in a bowl.
2. Mix well.
3. Stir in the shrimp and coat evenly with mixture.
4. Cover and marinate for 30 minutes.
5. Thread shrimp onto skewers.
6. Preheat your Pit Boss to 400 degrees F.
7. Add the shrimp to the griddle.
8. Grill for 3 minutes per side.

Honey Soy Salmon

Prep Time: 45 minutes
Cook Time: 6 minutes
Serve: 4

Ingredients:

- 1 teaspoon sesame oil
- 1 teaspoon chili paste
- 2 tablespoons ginger, minced
- 2 cloves garlic, grated
- 2 tablespoons lemon, juice
- 1 teaspoon honey
- 2 tablespoons soy sauce
- 4 salmon fillets

Directions:

1. Set your Pit Boss griddle to smoke.
2. Preheat it to 400 degrees F.
3. Add all ingredients except salmon to a bowl.
4. Mix well.
5. Add the salmon and coat evenly with marinade.
6. Refrigerate for 30 minutes.
7. Grill the salmon for 3 minutes per side.

Tuna Steak

Prep Time: 1 hour and 10 minutes
Cook Time: 20 minutes
Serve: 2

Ingredients:

- 2 tuna steaks
- Salt and pepper to taste
- ¼ cup lime juice
- 2 tablespoons rice wine vinegar
- 2 tablespoons sesame oil
- ½ cup soy sauce

Directions:

1. Preheat your Pit Boss griddle to 400 degrees F or to high heat.
2. Season the tuna with salt and pepper.
3. Mix the remaining ingredients in a bowl.
4. Add the tuna to the bowl.
5. Cover and marinate in the refrigerator for 1 hour.
6. Add to the griddle.
7. Cook for 45 minutes, turning every 15 minutes.

Shrimp Scampi

Prep Time: 15 minutes

Cook Time: 10 minutes

Serve: 3

Ingredients:

- ½ cup butter, sliced into cubes
- 3 cloves garlic, minced
- 2 teaspoons blackened rub seasoning
- ½ teaspoon red pepper flakes
- 1 ½ lb. shrimp, peeled and deveined
- 1 tablespoon lemon juice
- 1 teaspoon lemon zest
- 3 tablespoons parsley, chopped

Directions:

1. Preheat your Pit Boss griddle to medium high.
2. Add a pan on top of the griddle.
3. Add the butter.
4. Cook the garlic until fragrant.
5. Stir in the blackened rub seasoning and red pepper flakes.
6. Stir in the shrimp and cook for 2 minutes, stirring.
7. Mix the remaining ingredients in a bowl and add to the pan.
8. Simmer for 5 minutes and serve.

Fish Tacos

Prep Time: 10 minutes
Cook Time: 6 minutes
Serve: 12

Ingredients:

- 1 teaspoon garlic powder
- 1 teaspoon oregano
- 1 teaspoon black pepper
- ½ teaspoon cumin
- ¼ teaspoon cayenne pepper
- 1 ½ teaspoon paprika
- 1 ½ lb. cod fish

For assembling

- Tortillas
- Chopped lettuce
- Sour cream

Directions:

1. Preheat your Pit Boss griddle to 350 degrees F.
2. Mix the spices in a bowl.
3. Sprinkle fish with the spice mixture.
4. Grill for 3 minutes per side.
5. Top the tortillas with the fish, lettuce and sour cream.

Blackened Catfish

Prep Time: 30 minutes

Cook Time: 10 minutes

Serve: 4

Ingredients:

- ½ cup Cajun seasoning
- 1 teaspoon garlic, grated
- ¼ teaspoon cayenne pepper
- 1 teaspoon onion powder
- 1 teaspoon ground thyme
- 1 teaspoon pepper
- 1 teaspoon ground oregano
- 1 tablespoon smoked paprika
- 4 catfish fillets
- ½ cup butter

Directions:

1. Combine all the seasoning and spices in a bowl.
2. Sprinkle the fish with the spice mixture.
3. Marinate for 20 minutes.
4. Preheat your Pit Boss griddle to 450 degrees F or medium high heat.
5. Add a cast iron pan on the griddle.
6. Add the butter.
7. Cook the fish in the pan for 5 minutes per side.

Cajun Shrimp

Prep Time: 10 minutes

Cook Time: 15 minutes

Serve: 4

Ingredients:

- 2 tablespoons olive oil
- ½ lb. shrimp, peeled and deveined
- 1 tablespoon Cajun seasoning

Cajun Dip

- ½ cup mayonnaise
- 1 cup sour cream
- 1 teaspoon Cajun seasoning
- 1 clove garlic, minced
- 1 teaspoon lemon juice
- 1 tablespoon hot sauce

Directions:

1. Preheat your Pit Boss griddle to 350 degrees F or medium heat.
2. Brush shrimp with olive oil.
3. Season with the Cajun seasoning.
4. Grill for 15 minutes, turning every 5 minutes.
5. Mix the dip ingredients in a bowl.
6. Serve shrimp with dip.

Chapter 3: Pork Recipes

Chinese Barbecue Pork

Prep Time: 4 hours and 10 minutes
Cook Time: 20 minutes
Serve: 4

Ingredients:

- ¼ cup hoisin sauce
- 2 cloves garlic, minced
- ¼ cup barbecue sauce
- 1 tablespoon sugar
- 1 teaspoon sweet rib rub seasoning
- ¼ cup tamari
- ¼ cup white wine
- 2 lb. pork tenderloin, fat trimmed

Directions:

1. Combine all the ingredients except pork in a bowl.
2. Mix well.
3. Stir in the pork.
4. Cover and refrigerate for 4 hours.
5. Set your Pit Boss griddle to smoke.
6. Preheat it to 400 degrees F or medium high heat.
7. Add the pork on the griddle.
8. Cook for 5 minutes per side.
9. Brush with the marinade.
10. Cook for another 5 minutes per side.

Pulled Pork Tacos

Prep Time: 15 minutes
Cook Time: 5 minutes
Serve: 4

Ingredients:

- 4 tortillas
- 2 cups cooked pulled pork
- ½ cup radish, sliced into strips
- 1 white onion, chopped
- ¼ cup cucumber, chopped
- Chopped cilantro

Directions:

1. Preheat your Pit Boss griddle to 350 degrees F.
2. Top the tortillas with all the ingredients.
3. Fold and place on the griddle.
4. Grill for 1 to 2 minutes per side.

Greek Pork Skewers

Preparation Time: 10 minutes
Cooking Time: 10 minutes
Serve: 8

Ingredients:

- 2 lbs pork tenderloin, cut into cubes
- 1 onion, cut into chunks
- 2 bell pepper, cut into chunks

For marinade:

- 1/2 tsp ground coriander
- 1 tsp ground cumin
- 2 tbsp parsley, chopped
- 1 tbsp garlic, chopped
- 1/2 cup olive oil
- 1/2 cup vinegar
- 1/4 tsp pepper
- 1/2 tsp salt

Directions:

1. Add pork cubes and marinade ingredients into the zip-lock bag and mix well. The sealed bag shakes well and places in the refrigerator for 8 hours.
2. Thread marinated pork cubes, bell pepper, and onion onto the skewers.
3. Preheat the Pit Boss griddle to high heat.
4. Spray griddle top with cooking spray.
5. Place skewers on a hot griddle top and cooks for 10 minutes or an internal temperature of pork cubes reaches 145 F. Turn skewers 2-3 times.
6. Serve and enjoy.

Dijon Pork Skewers

Preparation Time: 10 minutes
Cooking Time: 12 minutes
Serve: 4

Ingredients:

- 1 1/2 lbs pork loin, cut into 1-inch cubes
- 2 cups mushrooms
- 2 cups cherry tomatoes
- 2 cups onion, cut into pieces
- 2 cups bell peppers, cut into pieces

For marinade:

- 1/2 cup vinaigrette
- 1/4 cup Dijon mustard
- Pepper
- Salt

Directions:

1. Add pork cubes and marinade ingredients into the mixing bowl and mix well and let it marinate for 30 minutes.
2. Thread marinated pork cubes, mushrooms, tomatoes, onion, and bell peppers onto the skewers.
3. Preheat the Pit Boss griddle to high heat.
4. Place skewers on a hot griddle top and cooks for 5-7 minutes on each side or until cooked through.
5. Serve and enjoy.

Flavors Balsamic Pork Chops

Preparation Time: 10 minutes
Cooking Time: 15 minutes
Serve: 4

Ingredients:

- 4 pork chops
- 1 tsp dried rosemary
- 1/8 tsp chili flakes
- 1/2 tsp pepper
- 1 tsp garlic, minced
- 2 tbsp Dijon mustard
- 3 tbsp olive oil
- 1/2 cup balsamic vinegar
- 3/4 tsp salt

Directions:

1. Add pork chops and remaining ingredients into the zip-lock bag. Seal bag, shake well and place in the refrigerator for 4 hours.
2. Preheat the Pit Boss griddle to medium heat.
3. Spray griddle top with cooking spray.
4. Place marinated pork chops on a hot griddle top and cook for 6-8 minutes on each side or until internal temperature reaches 145 F.
5. Serve and enjoy.

Maple Ham

Prep Time: 30 minutes

Cook Time: 3 hours

Serve: 12

Ingredients:

Glaze

- 3 tablespoons apple cider vinegar
- 1 ½ cups apple cider
- 2 tablespoons butter
- ½ cup brown sugar
- ½ cup maple syrup
- ¼ teaspoons chili powder
- 3 tablespoons Dijon mustard
- 2 teaspoons cornstarch
- ¼ teaspoon ground cloves
- ½ teaspoon ground cinnamon
- ¼ teaspoon dried thyme
- 2 teaspoon apple butter rub
- 3 tablespoons mustard

Ham

- 1 whole ham
- 1 cup water

Directions:

1. Preheat your Pit Boss griddle to 400 degrees F.
2. Add a cast iron pan to your grill.
3. Combine the glaze ingredients in the pan.
4. Mix well.
5. Bring to a boil.

6. Reduce grill temperature to 300 degrees F.
7. Simmer for 20 minutes, stirring every 5 to 6 minutes.
8. Remove from the griddle and set aside.
9. Add the ham to a baking pan.
10. Pour in the water and 1/3 of the glaze.
11. Cook for 2 hours.
12. Brush the ham with the glaze.
13. Grill for another 30 minutes or until caramelized.
14. Brush with the remaining glaze.
15. Grill for another 15 minutes.

Peppercorn Pork Chops

Prep Time: 15 minutes

Cook Time: 15 minutes

Serve: 4

Ingredients:

- 4 pork chops
- 1 teaspoon olive oil
- 1 tablespoon coriander
- 3 tablespoons peppercorns, ground
- 2 tablespoons sugar
- ¼ cup cumin
- 1 teaspoon dry rub
- Salt to taste

Directions:

1. Preheat your Pit Boss griddle to 450 degrees F.
2. Brush pork chops with olive oil.
3. Mix the remaining ingredients in a bowl.
4. Sprinkle both sides of pork chops with this mixture.
5. Grill the pork chops for 5 to 7 minutes per side.

Mustard Ribs

Prep Time: 20 minutes
Cook Time: 6 hours
Serve: 4

Ingredients:

- 2 cups yellow mustard
- 2 cups apple juice
- ¼ cup cider vinegar
- ¼ cup honey
- ¼ cup brown sugar
- 2 tablespoons ketchup
- 1 tablespoon hot sauce
- 1 tablespoon Worcestershire sauce
- 7 tablespoon sweet rib rub
- 1 rack ribs

Directions:

1. Combine all the ingredients except the ribs.
2. Mix well.
3. Coat ribs with the mixture.
4. Preheat your Pit Boss griddle to 275 degrees F.
5. Add the ribs to the griddle.
6. Grill for 3 hours, turning every 1 hour.
7. Brush with the sauce.
8. Grill for another 3 hours, flipping every 1 hour.

Stuffed Pork Chops

Prep Time: 30 minutes

Cook Time: 30 minutes

Serve: 4

Ingredients:

- 4 pork chops
- Pinch pulled pork seasoning
- 1 tablespoons parsley, chopped
- 1 white onion, chopped
- 1 pack hash browns, shredded
- ¼ cup sour cream
- 1 cup cheddar cheese, shredded

Directions:

1. Slice a pocket in the middle of the pork chops.
2. Sprinkle both sides of the pork chops with the seasoning.
3. In a bowl, mix the rest of the ingredients.
4. Stuff the pork chops with the mixture.
5. Preheat your Pit Boss griddle to 350 degrees F or medium heat.
6. Grill the pork chops for 30 minutes, flipping halfway through.

Pineapple Honey Pork Chops

Preparation Time: 10 minutes
Cooking Time: 12 minutes
Serve: 4

Ingredients:

- 4 pork chops, boneless
- 1 tbsp Dijon mustard
- 1/4 cup honey
- 8 oz crushed pineapple
- Pepper
- Salt

Directions:

1. Add pork chops and remaining ingredients into the zip-lock bag. Seal bag, shake well, and place in the refrigerator overnight.
2. Preheat the Pit Boss griddle to high heat.
3. Spray griddle top with cooking spray.
4. Place pork chops on a hot griddle top and cook for 5-6 minutes on each side.
5. Serve and enjoy.

Maple Meatballs

Prep Time: 15 minutes

Cook Time: 15 minutes

Serve: 4

Ingredients:

- 2 lb. ground pork
- 1 onion, grated
- 3 cloves garlic, minced
- 2 eggs, beaten
- 1 tablespoon maple syrup
- 1 tablespoon sweet heat rub
- 2 tablespoons milk

Directions:

1. Preheat your Pit Boss griddle to 350 degrees F or to medium heat.
2. Combine all the ingredients in a bowl.
3. Form meatballs from the mixture.
4. Add the meatballs to the griddle.
5. Cook for 15 minutes, turning three times.

Rosemary Pork Chops

Prep Time: 3 hours and 15 minutes

Cook Time: 10 minutes

Serve: 4

Ingredients:

- 1 cup soy sauce
- 6 tablespoons brown sugar
- 2 tablespoons dried rosemary
- ½ cup water
- 4 pork chops

Directions:

1. Combine soy sauce, brown sugar, rosemary and water in a bowl.
2. Add the pork chops and coat evenly with the sauce.
3. Cover and marinate for 3 hours.
4. Set your Pit Boss griddle to smoke.
5. Preheat it to 350 degrees F.
6. Grill the pork chops for 5 minutes per side.

Juicy Honey Soy Pork Chops

Preparation Time: 10 minutes
Cooking Time: 10 minutes
Serve: 6

Ingredients:

- 6 pork chops, boneless
- 1 tbsp vinegar
- 2 tbsp olive oil
- 1 tbsp soy sauce
- 1/4 cup honey
- Pepper
- Salt

Directions:

1. Add pork chops and remaining ingredients into the zip-lock bag and mix well. The sealed bag shakes well and places in the refrigerator for 2 hours.
2. Preheat the Pit Boss griddle to medium heat.
3. Spray griddle top with cooking spray.
4. Place pork chops on hot griddle top and cook for 5 minutes on each side or internal temperature reaches 145 F.
5. Serve and enjoy.

Grilled Pork Tenderloin

Prep Time: 1 hour and 10 minutes
Cook Time: 10 minutes
Serve: 4

Ingredients:

- 2 tablespoons olive oil
- 2 tablespoons brown sugar
- 2 tablespoons apple butter seasoning
- 1 pork tenderloin, fat trimmed

Directions:

1. Mix the olive oil, sugar and apple butter seasoning in a bowl.
2. Rub all sides of the pork tenderloin with the mixture.
3. Cover and marinate for 1 hour.
4. Set your Pit Boss griddle to smoke.
5. Preheat it to 350 degrees F.
6. Grill the pork for 5 minutes per side.

Breaded Pork Chops

Prep Time: 20 minutes
Cook Time: 6 minutes
Serve: 6

Ingredients:

- 6 pork chops
- Salt and pepper to taste
- 1 teaspoon dried rosemary
- ½ cup flour
- 1 ½ cup breadcrumbs
- ½ cup vegetable oil

Directions:

1. Season pork chops with salt and pepper.
2. Sprinkle with dried rosemary.
3. Coat with flour.
4. Dip in egg and dredge with breadcrumbs.
5. Add the oil to a pan.
6. Place the pan on top of the Pit Boss griddle.
7. Set the Pit Boss griddle to medium heat.
8. Cook the pork chops for 3 minutes per side or until golden.

Chapter 4: Beef Recipes

Beef Kefta

Prep Time: 1 hour and 10 minutes
Cook Time: 10 minutes
Serve: 4

Ingredients:

- 1 onion, grated
- 2 lb. ground beef
- 1 tablespoon blackened saskatchewan rub seasoning
- 3 tablespoon cilantro, chopped
- 1 teaspoon cumin
- 1 teaspoon paprika
- 3 tablespoon parsley, chopped

Directions:

1. Combine all the ingredients in a bowl.
2. Mix well.
3. Refrigerate for 1 hour.
4. Set your Pit Boss griddle to smoke.
5. Preheat it to 425 degrees F or medium high heat.
6. Shape the beef mixture into cylinders.
7. Grill the beef kefta for 5 minutes per side.

Roast Beef Sandwich

Preparation Time: 10 minutes
Cooking Time: 5 minutes
Serve: 1

Ingredients:

- 2 bread slices
- 2 cheese slices
- 4 deli roast beef, sliced
- 2 tsp butter
- 1 tbsp mayonnaise
- 1/4 cup caramelized onions, sliced

Directions:

1. Spread butter on one side of each bread slice.
2. Take 1 bread slice and spread with mayo top with beef, onion, and cheese.
3. Cover with remaining bread slice.
4. Preheat the Pit Boss griddle to high heat.
5. Spray griddle top with cooking spray.
6. Place sandwich on hot griddle top and cook for 5 minutes or until golden brown from both sides.
7. Serve and enjoy.

Dijon Beef Burger Patties

Preparation Time: 10 minutes
Cooking Time: 10 minutes
Serve: 4

Ingredients:

- 1 lb ground beef
- 1/2 tsp pepper
- 3/4 tbsp Worcestershire sauce
- 1 tbsp Dijon mustard
- 1/8 tsp cayenne
- 1/8 tsp chili flakes
- 1 tbsp parsley, chopped
- 1/2 tsp kosher salt

Directions:

1. Add all ingredients into the bowl and mix until well combined.
2. Preheat the Pit Boss griddle to high heat.
3. Spray griddle top with cooking spray.
4. Make patties from mixture and place on hot griddle top and cook for 5 minutes on each side.
5. Serve and enjoy.

Grilled Tomahawk Steak

Prep Time: 1 hour and 20 minutes
Cook Time: 45 minutes
Serve: 2

Ingredients:

- 2 tomahawk rib eye steaks
- Salt to taste
- 2 tablespoons steak seasoning
- 3 tablespoons butter
- 2 cloves garlic, minced
- 1 sprig rosemary, minced

Directions:

1. Preheat your Pit Boss griddle to 225 degrees F.
2. Season the steak with salt.
3. Let sit for 1 hour.
4. Seasons the steak with the steak seasoning.
5. Grill the steak for 45 minutes, turning once.
6. In a bowl, mix the butter, garlic and rosemary.
7. Top steak with the garlic butter and serve.

Korean Barbecue Short Ribs

Prep Time: 1 hour and 15 minutes
Cook Time: 4 hours
Serve: 4

Ingredients:

- ½ cup soy sauce
- 1 cup beef broth
- 1 tablespoon beef & brisket rub
- 1 tablespoon ginger, grated
- 3 cloves garlic, peeled
- 2 tablespoon brown sugar
- 4 beef short ribs
- 1 tablespoon sriracha sauce
- Toasted sesame seeds

Directions:

1. Mix soy sauce, broth, rub, ginger, garlic and sugar in a bowl.
2. Transfer to a sealable plastic.
3. Stir in the short ribs.
4. Marinate in the refrigerator for 1 hour.
5. Preheat your Pit Boss griddle to 250 degrees F.
6. Grill the ribs for 4 hours, turning several times.
7. Sprinkle with sesame seeds and serve.

Coffee Steak

Prep Time: 15 minutes
Cook Time: 35 minutes
Serve: 8

Ingredients:

- Garlic salt to taste
- Pinch instant coffee
- 4 rib eye steaks

Directions:

1. Rub garlic salt and coffee on both sides of steaks.
2. Set your Pit Boss griddle to smoke.
3. Preheat your grill to 350 degrees F.
4. Add the steaks to the griddle.
5. Smoke the steaks for 30 minutes.
6. Increase temperature to 375 degrees F.
7. Grill the steaks for 5 minutes.

Juicy Beef Burger Patties

Preparation Time: 10 minutes
Cooking Time: 12 minutes
Serve: 6

Ingredients:

- 2 lbs ground beef
- 2 tbsp Worcestershire sauce
- 3/4 cup onion, chopped
- 1/2 tsp pepper
- 1/2 tsp salt

Directions:

1. Add all ingredients into the bowl and mix until well combined.
2. Preheat the Pit Boss griddle to high heat.
3. Spray griddle top with cooking spray.
4. Make patties from mixture and place on hot griddle top and cook for 5 minutes on each side.
5. Serve and enjoy.

Mustard Prime Rib Roast

Prep Time: 15 minutes
Cook Time: 3 hours and 5 minutes
Serve: 8

Ingredients:

- 1 cup mustard
- 2 tablespoons garlic, minced
- 1 tablespoon salt
- 1 tablespoon pepper
- 1 prime rib roast

Directions:

1. Preheat your Pit Boss griddle to 450 degrees F.
2. Mix the mustard, garlic, salt and pepper in a bowl.
3. Rub the roast with the mixture.
4. Place the roast on top of the griddle.
5. Cover the griddle.
6. Cook for 45 minutes.
7. Reduce temperature to 325 degrees F.
8. Cook for another 2 hours and 30 minutes.

Beef Caldereta Stew

Prep Time: 40 minutes
Cook Time: 1 hour and 30 minutes
Serve: 12

Ingredients:

- 2 tablespoons olive oil
- 2 lb. beef chuck roast, sliced into cubes
- Salt to taste
- 4 cloves garlic, chopped
- 2 red bell peppers, sliced
- 2 green bell peppers, sliced
- 2 potatoes, diced
- 2 tablespoons tomato paste
- 2 cups tomato sauce
- 2 cups water
- ½ cup cheddar cheese, grated

Directions:

1. Preheat your Pit Boss griddle to 375 degrees F.
2. Add a cast iron pan on top of your grill.
3. Pour the oil into the pan.
4. Add the beef and cook until browned.
5. Season with salt.
6. Stir in the vegetables.
7. Cook while stirring for 5 minutes.
8. Add the tomato paste, tomato sauce and water.
9. Bring to a boil.
10. Reduce temperature to 275 degrees F.
11. Simmer for 1 hour.
12. Top with the cheese.
13. Cook for 2 more minutes and serve.

Beef Shawarma

Prep Time: 1 hour and 10 minutes
Cook Time: 10 minutes
Serve: 4

Ingredients:

- 1 ½ lbs flank steak
- 2 teaspoon olive oil
- 2 cloves garlic, minced
- 1 teaspoon paprika
- 1 ½ teaspoon ground coriander
- ½ teaspoon cayenne pepper
- ½ teaspoon ground cloves
- ½ teaspoon ground cinnamon

Directions:

1. Combine all the ingredients in a bowl.
2. Mix well.
3. Cover and refrigerate for 1 hour.
4. Preheat your Pit Boss griddle to 450 degrees F.
5. Grill the steaks for 5 minutes per side.
6. Transfer to a cutting board.
7. Slice across the grain.

Herbed Prime Rib Steak

Prep Time: 12 hours and 15 minutes
Cook Time: 2 hours and 30 minutes
Serve: 4

Ingredients:

- 1/3 cup olive oil
- 6 cloves garlic
- 3 tablespoons fresh thyme
- 3 tablespoons fresh rosemary
- Pinch steak seasoning
- 7 lb. prime rib roast

Directions:

1. Add the olive oil, garlic, herbs and seasoning in a food processor.
2. Pulse until smooth.
3. Coat the prime rib with the paste.
4. Cover and refrigerate for 12 hours.
5. Preheat your Pit Boss griddle to 250 degrees F.
6. Grill the prime rib for 2 hours.
7. Increase temperature to 400 degrees F.
8. Grill for 15 to 30 minutes.

Rib Eye Steak with Herb Butter

Prep Time: 1 day and 10 minutes
Cook Time: 1 hour
Serve: 2

Ingredients:

Herb butter

- ¼ cup butter
- 1 teaspoon horseradish
- 1 tablespoon parsley, chopped

Marinade

- ¼ cup olive oil
- 2 cloves garlic, minced
- ¼ cup red wine
- 2 teaspoon pepper
- 1 tablespoon Dijon mustard
- 1 tablespoon red wine vinegar
- 1 tablespoon dried rosemary
- 1 teaspoon Worcestershire sauce

Steak

- 2 rib eye steaks

Directions:

1. Mix the herb butter ingredients in a small bowl.
2. Cover and refrigerate.
3. Combine the marinade ingredients in a sealable plastic bag.
4. Add the steaks and turn to coat evenly.
5. Marinate in the refrigerator overnight.
6. Set your Pit Boss griddle to smoke.
7. Preheat your grill to 350 degrees F.

8. Add the steaks to the griddle.
9. Smoke for 40 to 50 minutes.
10. Increase temperature to 375 degrees F.
11. Grill the steaks for 15 minutes.
12. Add the herb butter on top and serve.

Steak Tips

Prep Time: 15 minutes
Cook Time: 15 minutes
Serve: 4

Ingredients:

- 2 lb. strip sirloin steak
- 4 tablespoons steak seasoning
- ¼ cup butter
- 1 tablespoon garlic, minced

Directions:

1. Season the steaks with the steak seasoning.
2. Preheat your Pit Boss griddle to 375 degrees F.
3. Grill the steaks for 5 to 7 minutes per side.
4. Transfer to a cutting board and slice into strips.
5. In a pan over medium heat, melt the butter and cook the garlic until fragrant.
6. Drizzle steak tips with butter sauce.

Pineapple Beef Burger Patties

Preparation Time: 10 minutes
Cooking Time: 8 minutes
Serve: 4

Ingredients:

- 1 1/4 lbs ground beef
- 2 pineapple slices, chopped
- 1/4 tsp pepper
- 1 garlic clove, minced
- 1 tsp ginger, grated
- 1/4 cup green onions, chopped
- 1/4 cup soy sauce
- Salt

Directions:

1. Add all ingredients into the bowl and mix until well combined.
2. Preheat the Pit Boss griddle to high heat.
3. Spray griddle top with cooking spray.
4. Make patties from mixture and place on hot griddle top and cook for 4 minutes on each side.
5. Serve and enjoy.

Tomato Roast Beef Sandwich

Preparation Time: 10 minutes
Cooking Time: 10 minutes
Serve: 2

Ingredients:

- 4 bread slices
- 1/2 lb deli roast beef slices
- 2 tbsp mayonnaise
- 1 tbsp butter
- 1/2 onion, sliced
- 1 tomato, sliced
- 4 cheese slices

Directions:

1. Spread butter on one side of each bread slice.
2. Take 4 bread slices and spread with mayo and top with beef, cheese, tomatoes, and onion.
3. Cover with remaining bread slices.
4. Preheat the Pit Boss griddle to high heat.
5. Spray griddle top with cooking spray.
6. Place sandwich on hot griddle top and cook for 5 minutes or until golden brown from both sides.
7. Serve and enjoy.

Chapter 5: Vegetable Recipes

Garlic Potatoes

Prep Time: 10 minutes

Cook Time: 30 minutes

Serve: 6

Ingredients:

- 4 red potatoes, sliced
- 3 tablespoons butter, melted
- 1 onion, sliced
- 3 cloves garlic, minced

Directions:

1. Preheat your Pit Boss griddle to 400 degrees F.
2. Spread the potatoes in a baking pan.
3. Stir in the rest of the ingredients.
4. Cover the pan with foil.
5. Cook on the griddle for 30 minutes or until tender.

Green Chili Mashed Potatoes

Prep Time: 20 minutes
Cook Time: 40 minutes
Serve: 4

Ingredients:

- 3 lb. potatoes, sliced in half
- Water
- ½ cup green chili
- ½ cup butter
- Pinch smoked rub
- ¼ milk
- 2 tablespoons smoked seasoning

Directions:

1. Boil the potatoes in a pot with water.
2. Cook until tender.
3. Drain the potatoes.
4. Preheat your Pit Boss griddle to 350 degrees F.
5. Add the potatoes on top of the griddle.
6. Add the green chili beside the potatoes.
7. Cook for 10 minutes.
8. Transfer to a plate and let cool.
9. Transfer to a food processor along with the rest of the ingredients.
10. Process until smooth.

Chili Verde Sauce

Prep Time: 15 minutes
Cook Time: 10 minutes
Serve: 4

Ingredients:

- 1 onion, sliced
- 3 cloves garlic, peeled
- 4 serrano chili pepper
- 1 lb. tomatillos, husked
- ¼ cup olive oil, divided
- 1 tablespoon sweet heat rub
- 1 cup cilantro

Directions:

1. Drizzle the onion, garlic, chili pepper and tomatillos with 2 tablespoons olive oil.
2. Set the Pit Boss griddle to 375 degrees F.
3. Grill for 5 to 10 minutes.
4. Transfer to a plate and let cool.
5. Add grilled veggies to a food processor along with the remaining ingredients.
6. Process until smooth.

Asparagus with Bacon

Prep Time: 10 minutes

Cook Time: 30 minutes

Serve: 4

Ingredients:

- 1 bunch asparagus
- Bacon slices

Directions:

1. Preheat your Pit Boss griddle to 400 degrees F.
2. Wrap each asparagus spear with bacon slice.
3. Place on the griddle.
4. Grill for 25 minutes, turning once or twice.

Mexican Corn Salad

Prep Time: 10 minutes
Cook Time: 10 minutes
Serve: 4

Ingredients:

- 1 tablespoon cilantro, chopped
- 4 cobs corn
- 1 tablespoon lime juice
- 1 tablespoon chicken seasoning
- 1 teaspoon paprika
- ¼ cup sour cream
- 2 tablespoon mayo
- ½ cup feta cheese, crumbled

Directions:

1. Preheat your Pit Boss griddle to 350 degrees F.
2. Grill the corn for 10 minutes, turning several times.
3. Slice off the corn kernels and add to a bowl.
4. Stir in the rest of the ingredients.

Southern Green Beans

Prep Time: 15 minutes
Cook Time: 1 hour and 15 minutes
Serve: 6

Ingredients:

- 4 slices bacon
- 1 tablespoon butter
- 2 lb. green beans, trimmed
- 2 cups water
- 2 cups chicken broth
- Pinch hickory bacon seasoning

Directions:

1. Preheat your Pit Boss griddle to 350 degrees F or medium heat.
2. Add a cast iron skillet on top of the griddle.
3. Add the bacon and cook for 15 minutes.
4. Transfer the bacon to a plate.
5. Add the rest of the ingredients to the pan.
6. Close the griddle lid.
7. Cook for 1 hour.
8. While waiting, chop the bacon.
9. Sprinkle chopped bacon on top of the green beans and serve.

Grilled Pickles with Bacon

Prep Time: 10 minutes

Cook Time: 45 minutes

Serve: 6

Ingredients:

- 13 strips bacon
- 13 spears dill pickles

Directions:

1. Preheat your Pit Boss griddle to 375 degrees F.
2. Wrap the dill pickles with the bacon.
3. Secure with a toothpick.
4. Grill for 45 minutes, turning several times.

Cheesy Potato Casserole

Prep Time: 15 minutes
Cook Time: 1 hour and 30 minutes
Serve: 15

Ingredients:

- Cooking spray
- 32 oz. potatoes, sliced
- 1 can cream of mushroom soup
- 1 can cream of celery soup
- 1 1lb. cheese sauce
- 8 oz. sour cream
- Pinch steak seasoning

Directions:

1. Preheat your Pit Boss griddle to 350 degrees F.
2. Spray your baking pan with oil.
3. Spread potatoes in the baking pan.
4. Mix the remaining ingredients in a bowl.
5. Top the potatoes with this mixture.
6. Cover with foil.
7. Cook on top of the griddle for 1 hour.
8. Remove foil and cook for 30 more minutes.

Mashed Potato Cakes

Prep Time: 40 minutes

Cook Time: 10 minutes

Serve: 6

Ingredients:

- 3 cups mashed potatoes
- ½ cup bacon bits, cooked
- 1 egg, beaten
- 1 cup cheddar jack cheese, shredded
- 1 teaspoon hickory bacon rub
- 1/3 cup flour
- 4 scallions, minced
- 2 tablespoons butter
- 2 teaspoons mustard

Directions:

1. Combine all the ingredients in a bowl.
2. Form balls from the mixture.
3. Flatten the balls to form the patties.
4. Add the potato cakes on top of the griddle.
5. Cook over medium low heat for 3 minutes per side or until golden.

Grilled Cauliflower Salad

Prep Time: 15 minutes

Cook Time: 10 minutes

Serve: 6

Ingredients:

- 1 head cauliflower, sliced into 4 portions
- 1 tablespoon olive oil
- 1 cup mayonnaise
- 1 cup sour cream
- 2 tablespoons brown mustard
- 8 hard-boiled eggs, peeled and sliced
- ½ cup bacon, cooked and crumbled
- ¼ cup parsley, chopped
- 3 scallions, chopped
- Garlic salt to taste

Directions:

1. Drizzle cauliflower with olive oil.
2. Preheat your Pit Boss griddle to 375 degrees F.
3. Grill the cauliflower for 5 minutes per side.
4. Separate into florets and place in a bowl.
5. Stir in the rest of the ingredients.

Chapter 6: Vegetarian/Vegan Recipes

Corn with Cilantro & Lime

Prep Time: 10 minutes

Cook Time: 20 minutes

Serve: 4

Ingredients:

- 2 tablespoons butter, melted
- ½ cup cilantro, chopped
- 4 cobs corn
- 2 tablespoons lime juice

Directions:

1. Preheat your Pit Boss griddle to 400 degrees F.
2. Grill the corn for 15 minutes, rotating often.
3. Brush the corn with butter.
4. Sprinkle with the cilantro and drizzle with lime juice.

Grilled Mushrooms

Prep Time: 10 minutes
Cook Time: 15 minutes
Serve: 4

Ingredients:

- 4 large Portobello mushrooms
- 1 tablespoon olive oil
- 1 teaspoon garlic salt
- 2 tablespoons parsley, chopped

Directions:

1. Drizzle mushrooms with oil.
2. Sprinkle with garlic salt.
3. Set your Pit Boss griddle to 375 degrees F.
4. Cook for 15 minutes, turning twice.
5. Sprinkle with parsley before serving.

Roasted Bell Peppers

Prep Time: 10 minutes

Cook Time: 10 minutes

Serve: 4

Ingredients:

- 1 red bell pepper, sliced in half
- 1 yellow bell pepper, sliced in half
- 1 green bell pepper, sliced in half
- 1 orange bell pepper, sliced in half
- Olive oil
- Salt and pepper to taste

Directions:

1. Preheat your Pit Boss griddle to 350 degrees F.
2. Drizzle bell peppers with oil.
3. Season with salt and pepper.
4. Add to the griddle.
5. Grill for 3 to 5 minutes per side.

Pineapple Slices

Preparation Time: 10 minutes
Cooking Time: 8 minutes
Serve: 6

Ingredients:

- 6 pineapple slices
- 1/4 tsp chili powder
- 1 tsp cinnamon
- 2 tbsp honey
- Pinch of salt

Directions:

1. Season pineapple slices with chili powder, cinnamon, and salt and brush with honey.
2. Preheat the Pit Boss griddle to medium heat.
3. Place pineapple slices on a hot griddle top and cook until lightly browned from both sides.
4. Serve and enjoy.

Tofu & Vegetable Kebab

Prep Time: 15 minutes

Cook Time: 15 minutes

Serve: 4

Ingredients:

- 1 block tofu, sliced into cubes
- 1 white onion, sliced
- 1 red bell pepper, sliced
- 1 green bell pepper, sliced
- Olive oil
- ¼ teaspoon cumin
- ½ teaspoon garlic powder

Directions:

1. Preheat your Pit Boss griddle to 350 degrees F.
2. Thread tofu and vegetables alternately onto skewers.
3. Drizzle with oil and season with cumin and garlic powder.
4. Grill for 10 to 15 minutes, rotating frequently.

Lemon Garlic Tofu

Prep Time: 10 minutes

Cook Time: 10 minutes

Serve: 4

Ingredients:

- 1 block tofu, sliced
- 1 tablespoon olive oil
- 1 tablespoon lemon juice
- 1 teaspoon garlic powder
- Pepper to taste

Directions:

1. Drizzle tofu with a mix of olive oil and lemon juice.
2. Sprinkle with garlic powder and pepper.
3. Place on the Pit Boss griddle.
4. Set it to 375 degrees F.
5. Grill for 5 minutes per side.

Cowboy Beans

Prep Time: 10 minutes

Cook Time: 3 hours

Serve: 8

Ingredients:

- 1 cup barbecue sauce
- 10 oz. canned diced tomatoes with green chili
- 6 cloves garlic, minced
- 2 jalapeno peppers, chopped
- Salt to taste
- 1 lb. pinto beans, dried
- 1 tablespoon Worcestershire sauce
- 1 yellow onion, chopped
- Water

Directions:

1. Preheat your Pit Boss griddle to 400 degrees F or medium high heat.
2. Add all the ingredients to your Dutch oven and place it on top of the griddle.
3. Bring to a boil.
4. Cover the pot and reduce temperature to 300 degrees F.
5. Cook for 1 hour.
6. Reduce temperature to 275 degrees F and cook for 2 hours.

Tomato Basil Sandwich

Preparation Time: 10 minutes
Cooking Time: 5 minutes
Serve: 1

Ingredients:

- 2 bread slices
- 1 onion sliced
- 1 tomato, sliced
- 1 tbsp butter
- 4 fresh basil leaves
- 1/2 cup mozzarella cheese, shredded

Directions:

1. Spread butter on one side of each bread slice.
2. Take 1 bread slice and top with tomato, onion, basil, and cheese.
3. Cover with remaining bread slice.
4. Preheat the Pit Boss griddle to high heat.
5. Spray griddle top with cooking spray.
6. Place sandwich on hot griddle top and cook for 5 minutes or until lightly golden brown from both sides.
7. Serve and enjoy.

Grilled Zucchini

Prep Time: 10 minutes
Cook Time: 30 minutes
Serve: 4

Ingredients:

- 2 zucchinis, sliced in half lengthwise
- Olive oil
- Pinch garlic salt

Directions:

1. Drizzle zucchini with olive oil.
2. Season with garlic salt.
3. Add to the Pit Boss griddle.
4. Set the griddle to 375 degrees F.
5. Grill for 10 to 15 minutes per side.

Sweet Potato Casserole

Prep Time: 10 minutes

Cook Time: 1 hour and 30 minutes

Serve: 4

Ingredients:

- ¼ cup brown sugar
- ¼ cup vegan butter
- 4 oz. pecans, chopped
- ½ teaspoon cinnamon
- 2 teaspoons apple butter rub
- 4 sweet potatoes, sliced

Directions:

1. Preheat your Pit Boss griddle to 350 degrees F or medium high heat.
2. Combine all the ingredients in a baking pan.
3. Cover the pan with foil.
4. Add to the griddle.
5. Cook for 1 hour.
6. Increase temperature to 375 degrees F.
7. Cook for another 30 minutes.

Squash with Pesto

Preparation Time: 10 minutes
Cooking Time: 10 minutes
Serve: 6

Ingredients:

- 6 small summer squash, sliced
- Pepper
- Salt

For pesto:

- 1/4 cup pecorino romano, grated
- 1 cup basil leaves
- 1 garlic clove
- 1/4 cup pistachios
- 1/4 cup olive oil
- 1/4 tsp chili flakes
- Pepper
- Salt

Directions:

1. Preheat the Pit Boss griddle to high heat.
2. Season summer squash with pepper and salt and place on hot griddle top and cook for 4-5 minutes on each side.
3. Add all pesto ingredients into the blender and blend until smooth.
4. Pour pesto over cooked summer squash and serve.

Potato Patties

Preparation Time: 10 minutes
Cooking Time: 10 minutes
Serve: 5

Ingredients:

- 1 egg
- 2 cups mashed potatoes
- 2 tbsp parsley, chopped
- 2 tbsp basil, chopped
- 1/2 cup flour
- 2 garlic cloves, minced
- 1/4 cup green onion, chopped
- 1/2 onion, diced
- 1 tbsp Worcestershire sauce
- 1 cup cheddar cheese, shredded
- Pepper
- Salt

Directions:

1. Add all ingredients into the mixing bowl and mix until well combined.
2. Preheat the Pit Boss griddle to high heat.
3. Spray griddle top with cooking spray.
4. Make patties from mixture and place on hot griddle top and cook until lightly browned from both sides.
5. Serve and enjoy.

Sweet Potato Medley

Prep Time: 15 minutes

Cook Time: 45 minutes

Serve: 8

Ingredients:

- 8 Brussels sprouts, sliced in half
- 2 sweet potatoes, diced
- 3 tablespoons olive oil
- ½ white onion, sliced
- 1 red bell pepper, sliced
- Lemon pepper seasoning

Directions:

1. Toss the ingredients in a baking pan.
2. Cover with foil.
3. Add to the griddle.
4. Set your Pit Boss griddle to 450 degrees F.
5. Cook for 45 minutes, stirring once.

Lemon Garlic Green Beans

Prep Time: 10 minutes
Cook Time: 20 minutes
Serve: 6

Ingredients:

- 1 lb. green beans, trimmed
- 5 tablespoons butter, melted
- 3 cloves garlic, minced
- Pepper to taste
- Pinch lemon pepper garlic seasoning

Directions:

1. Set your Pit Boss griddle to smoke.
2. Preheat it to 350 degrees F.
3. Toss all ingredients in a baking pan.
4. Cover pan with foil.
5. Place the pan on top of the griddle.
6. Grill for 20 minutes.

Stir Fry Zucchini & Carrots

Preparation Time: 10 minutes
Cooking Time: 10 minutes
Serve: 4

Ingredients:

- 2 zucchinis, sliced
- 1 tsp garlic powder
- 1 tsp dried parsley
- 1 tsp dried thyme
- 3 carrots, sliced
- 2 tbsp olive oil
- 1/2 tsp dried oregano
- Pepper
- Salt

Directions:

1. Add zucchini, carrots, and remaining ingredients into the mixing bowl and toss well.
2. Preheat the Pit Boss griddle to high heat.
3. Spray griddle top with cooking spray.
4. Place zucchini and carrot mixture on hot griddle top and cook for 8-10 minutes.
5. Serve and enjoy.

Conclusion

Do you want to prepare fantastic meals effortlessly in outdoor camping and other picnic, party celebration activities? Have you used your Pit Boss gas griddle to the fullest and discover delicious recipes for your griddle cooking? If you answered "Yes", you're in the right place!

Get more about the secret of delicious food with PIT BOSS Gas Griddle Cookbook for Beginners 2021. With professional advice on how to use your Pit Boss gas griddle to the fullest, you can take your barbecue skill to the next level and use it for virtually any recipe!

Lightning Source UK Ltd.
Milton Keynes UK
UKHW050638260821
389520UK00007B/471